Oliver Goldsmith, M. M. Taylor

The Traveller

Oliver Goldsmith, M. M. Taylor

The Traveller

ISBN/EAN: 9783337292904

Printed in Europe, USA, Canada, Australia, Japan

Cover: Foto ©Thomas Meinert / pixelio.de

More available books at **www.hansebooks.com**

THE TRAVELLER.

THE TRAVELLER.

BY

OLIVER GOLDSMITH.

WITH ETCHINGS

BY

M. M. TAYLOR.

PHILADELPHIA:

J. B. LIPPINCOTT COMPANY.

1889.

LIST OF ILLUSTRATIONS.

THE TRAVELLER.

REMOTE, unfriended, melancholy, slow,
Or by the lazy Scheld, or wandering Po;
Or onward, where the rude Carinthian boor
Against the houseless stranger shuts the door;
Or where Campania's plain forsaken lies,
A weary waste expanding to the skies;
Where'er I roam, whatever realms to see,
My heart, untravelled, fondly turns to thee;
Still to my brother turns, with ceaseless pain,
And drags at each remove a lengthening chain.

Eternal blessings crown my earliest friend,
And round his dwelling guardian saints attend!
Blest be that spot, where cheerful guests retire
To pause from toil and trim their evening fire!
Blest that abode, where want and pain repair,
And every stranger finds a ready chair!
Blest be those feasts with simple plenty crowned,
Where all the ruddy family around

Laugh at the jests or pranks that never fail,
Or sigh with pity at some mournful tale,
Or press the bashful stranger to his food,
And learn the luxury of doing good!

But me, not destined such delights to share,
My prime of life in wandering spent and care,
Impelled with steps unceasing to pursue
Some fleeting good, that mocks me with the view,
That, like the circle bounding earth and skies,
Allures from far, yet, as I follow, flies:
My fortune leads to traverse realms alone,
And find no spot of all the world my own.

E'en now, where Alpine solitudes ascend,
I sit me down a pensive hour to spend,
And, placed on high above the storm's career,
Look downward where a hundred realms appear:
Lakes, forests, cities, plains extending wide,
The pomp of kings, the shepherd's humbler pride.

When thus creation's charms around combine,
Amidst the store should thankless pride repine?
Say, should the philosophic mind disdain
That good which makes each humbler bosom vain?

11

Let school-taught pride dissemble all it can,
These little things are great to little man;
And wiser he whose sympathetic mind
Exults in all the good of all mankind.
Ye glittering towns, with wealth and splendor crowned;
Ye fields, where summer spreads profusion round;
Ye lakes, whose vessels catch the busy gale;
Ye bending swains, that dress the flowery vale;
For me your tributary stores combine,
Creation's heir, the world—the world is mine!

As some lone miser, visiting his store,
Bends at his treasure, counts, recounts it o'er;
Hoards after hoards his rising raptures fill,
Yet still he sighs, for hoards are wanting still:
Thus to my breast alternate passions rise,
Pleased with each good that Heaven to man supplies;
Yet oft a sigh prevails, and sorrows fall,
To see the hoard of human bliss so small;
And oft I wish, amidst the scene, to find
Some spot to real happiness consigned,
Where my worn soul, each wandering hope at rest,
May gather bliss to see my fellows blest.

M.H.Taylor

But where to find that happiest spot below,
Who can direct, when all pretend to know?
The shuddering tenant of the frigid zone
Boldly proclaims that happiest spot his own,
Extols the treasures of his stormy seas,
And his long nights of revelry and ease;
The naked negro, panting at the line,
Boasts of his golden sands and palmy wine,
Basks in the glare, or stems the tepid wave,
And thanks his gods for all the good they gave.

Such is the patriot's boast, where'er we roam,
His first, best country ever is at home.
And yet, perhaps, if countries we compare,
And estimate the blessings which they share,
Though patriots flatter, still shall wisdom find
An equal portion dealt to all mankind;
As different good by art or nature given
To different nations makes their blessings even.

Nature, a mother kind alike to all,
Still grants her bliss at labor's earnest call;
With food as well the peasant is supplied
On Idra's cliffs as Arno's shelvy side;

15

And though the rocky crested summits frown,
These rocks, by custom, turn to beds of down.
From art more various are the blessings sent,—
Wealth, commerce, honor, liberty, content.
Yet these each other's power so strong contest,
That either seems destructive of the rest.
Where wealth and freedom reign, contentment fails,
And honor sinks where commerce long prevails.
Hence every state, to one loved blessing prone,
Conforms and models life to that alone.
Each to the favorite happiness attends,
And spurns the plan that aims at other ends;
Till, carried to excess in each domain,
This favorite good begets peculiar pain.

But let us try these truths with closer eyes,
And trace them through the prospect as it lies:
Here, for a while, my proper cares resigned,
Here let me sit in sorrow for mankind,
Like yon neglected shrub, at random cast,
That shades the steep, and sighs at every blast.

Far to the right, where Apennine ascends,
Bright as the summer, Italy extends:

c   17

Its uplands sloping deck the mountain's side,
Woods over woods in gay theatric pride;
While oft some temple's mouldering tops between
With venerable grandeur mark the scene.

Could nature's bounty satisfy the breast,
The sons of Italy were surely blest.
Whatever fruits in different climes are found,
That proudly rise, or humbly court the ground;
Whatever blooms in torrid tracts appear,
Whose bright succession decks the varied year;
Whatever sweets salute the northern sky
With vernal lives, that blossom but to die;
These, here disporting, own the kindred soil,
Nor ask luxuriance from the planter's toil;
While sea-born gales their gelid wings expand
To winnow fragrance round the smiling land.

But small the bliss that sense alone bestows,
And sensual bliss is all the nation knows.
In florid beauty groves and fields appear,
Man seems the only growth that dwindles here.
Contrasted faults through all his manners reign:
Though poor, luxurious; though submissive, vain;

Though grave, yet trifling; zealous, yet untrue;
And e'en in penance planning sins anew.
All evils here contaminate the mind,
That opulence departed leaves behind ;
For wealth was theirs, not far removed the date,
When commerce proudly flourished through the state ;
At her command the palace learned to rise,
Again the long-fall'n column sought the skies,
The canvas glowed beyond e'en nature warm,
The pregnant quarry teemed with human form ;
Till, more unsteady than the southern gale,
Commerce on other shores displayed her sail ;
While naught remained of all that riches gave,
But towns unmanned, and lords without a slave ;
And late the nation found, with fruitless skill,
Its former strength was but plethoric ill.

Yet still the loss of wealth is here supplied
By arts, the splendid wrecks of former pride ;
From these the feeble heart and long-fall'n mind
An easy compensation seem to find.
Here may be seen, in bloodless pomp arrayed,
The pasteboard triumph and the cavalcade ;

Processions formed for piety and love,
A mistress or a saint in every grove.
By sports like these are all their cares beguiled;
The sports of children satisfy the child;
Each nobler aim, represt by long control,
Now sinks at last, or feebly mans the soul;
While low delights, succeeding fast behind,
In happier meanness occupy the mind:
As in those domes, where Cæsars once bore sway,
Defaced by time and tottering in decay,
There in the ruin, heedless of the dead,
The shelter-seeking peasant builds his shed,
And, wondering man could want the larger pile,
Exults, and owns his cottage with a smile.

My soul, turn from them, turn we to survey
Where rougher climes a nobler race display,
Where the bleak Swiss their stormy mansion tread,
And force a churlish soil for scanty bread;
No product here the barren hills afford
But man and steel, the soldier and his sword;
No vernal blooms their torpid rocks array,
But winter lingering chills the lap of May;

23

No zephyr fondly sues the mountain's breast,
But meteors glare, and stormy glooms invest.

Yet still, even here, content can spread a charm,
Redress the clime, and all its rage disarm.
Though poor the peasant's hut, his feasts though small,
He sees his little lot the lot of all;
Sees no contiguous palace rear its head,
To shame the meanness of his humble shed;
No costly lord the sumptuous banquet deal,
To make him loathe his vegetable meal;
But calm, and bred in ignorance and toil,
Each wish contracting, fits him to the soil.
Cheerful, at morn, he wakes from short repose,
Breathes the keen air, and carols as he goes;
With patient angle trolls the finny deep;
Or drives his venturous ploughshare to the steep;
Or seeks the den where snow-tracks mark the way,
And drags the struggling savage into day.
At night returning, every labor sped,
He sits him down the monarch of a shed,
Smiles by his cheerful fire, and round surveys
His children's looks, that brighten at the blaze;

While his loved partner, boastful of her hoard,
Displays her cleanly platter on the board;
And haply too some pilgrim, thither led,
With many a tale repays the nightly bed.

Thus every good his native wilds impart
Imprints the patriot passion on his heart;
And e'en those ills that round his mansion rise
Enhance the bliss his scanty fund supplies;
Dear is that shed to which his soul conforms,
And dear that hill which lifts him to the storms;
And as a child, when scaring sounds molest,
Clings close and closer to the mother's breast,
So the loud torrent, and the whirlwind's roar,
But bind him to his native mountains more.

Such are the charms to barren states assigned:
Their wants but few, their wishes all confined.
Yet, let them only share the praises due,
If few their wants, their pleasures are but few;
For every want that stimulates the breast
Becomes a source of pleasure when redrest.
Whence from such lands each pleasing science flies,
That first excites desire, and then supplies;

Unknown to them, when sensual pleasures cloy,
To fill the languid pause with finer joy;
Unknown those powers that raise the soul to flame,
Catch every nerve, and vibrate through the frame.
Their level life is but a smouldering fire,
Unquenched by want, unfanned by strong desire;
Unfit for raptures, or, if raptures cheer
On some high festival of once a year,
In wild excess the vulgar breast takes fire,
Till, buried in debauch, the bliss expire.

But not their joys alone thus coarsely flow:
Their morals, like their pleasures, are but low;
For, as refinement stops, from sire to son,
Unaltered, unimproved, the manners run,
And love's and friendship's finely-pointed dart
Fall blunted from each indurated heart.
Some sterner virtues o'er the mountain's breast
May sit, like falcons cowering on the nest;
But all the gentler morals, such as play
Through life's more cultured walks and charm the way,
These, far dispersed, on timorous pinions fly,
To sport and flutter in a kinder sky.

To kinder skies, where gentler manners reign,
I turn; and France displays her bright domain.
Gay, sprightly land of mirth and social ease,
Pleased with thyself, whom all the world can please,
How often have I led thy sportive choir,
With tuneless pipe, beside the murmuring Loire!
Where shading elms along the margin grew,
And freshened from the wave the zephyr flew;
And haply though my harsh touch, faltering still,
But mocked all tune, and marred the dancers' skill,
Yet would the village praise my wondrous power,
And dance, forgetful of the noontide hour.
Alike all ages. Dames of ancient days
Have led their children through the mirthful maze,
And the gay grandsire, skilled in gestic lore,
Has frisked beneath the burthen of threescore.

So a blest life these thoughtless realms display;
Thus idly busy rolls their world away:
Theirs are those arts that mind to mind endear,
For honor forms the social temper here;
Honor, that praise which real merit gains,
Or even imaginary worth obtains,

31

Here passes current; paid from hand to hand,
It shifts in splendid traffic round the land;
From courts to camps, to cottages it strays,
And all are taught an avarice of praise:
They please, are pleased; they give to get esteem,
Till, seeming blest, they grow to what they seem.

But while this softer art their bliss supplies,
It gives their follies also room to rise;
For praise too dearly loved or warmly sought
Enfeebles all internal strength of thought,
And the weak soul, within itself unblest,
Leans for all pleasure on another's breast.
Hence ostentation here, with tawdry art,
Pants for the vulgar praise which fools impart;
Here vanity assumes her pert grimace,
And trims her robes of frieze with copper lace;
Here beggar pride defrauds her daily cheer,
To boast one splendid banquet once a year:
The mind still turns where shifting fashion draws,
Nor weighs the solid worth of self-applause.

To men of other minds my fancy flies,
Embosomed in the deep where Holland lies.

Methinks her patient sons before me stand,

Where the broad ocean leans against the land,

And, sedulous to stop the coming tide,

Lift the tall rampire's artificial pride.

Onward, methinks, and diligently slow,

The firm connected bulwark seems to grow,

Spreads its long arms amidst the watery roar,

Scoops out an empire, and usurps the shore;

While the pent ocean, rising o'er the pile,

Sees an amphibious world beneath him smile;

The slow canal, the yellow-blossomed vale,

The willow-tufted bank, the gliding sail,

The crowded mart, the cultivated plain,

A new creation rescued from his reign.

Thus, while around the wave-subjected soil

Impels the native to repeated toil,

Industrious habits in each bosom reign,

And industry begets a love of gain.

Hence all the good from opulence that springs,

With all those ills superfluous treasure brings,

Are here displayed. Their much-loved wealth imparts

Convenience, plenty, elegance, and arts;

But view them closer, craft and fraud appear,
Even liberty itself is bartered here.
At gold's superior charms all freedom flies;
The needy sell it, and the rich man buys:
A land of tyrants, and a den of slaves,
Here wretches seek dishonorable graves,
And, calmly bent, to servitude conform,
Dull as their lakes that slumber in the storm.

Heavens! how unlike their Belgic sires of old,
Rough, poor, content, ungovernably bold,
War in each breast, and freedom on each brow!
How much unlike the sons of Britain now!

Fired at the sound, my genius spreads her wing,
And flies where Britain courts the western spring;
Where lawns extend that scorn Arcadian pride,
And brighter streams than famed Hydaspes glide.
There, all around, the gentlest breezes stray;
There gentle music melts on every spray;
Creation's mildest charms are there combined:
Extremes are only in the master's mind.
Stern o'er each bosom reason holds her state,
With daring aims irregularly great.

37

Pride in their port, defiance in their eye,
I see the lords of human kind pass by,
Intent on high designs, a thoughtful band,
By forms unfashioned, fresh from nature's hand,
Fierce in their native hardiness of soul,
True to imagined right, above control;
While e'en the peasant boasts these rights to scan,
And learns to venerate himself as man.

Thine, Freedom, thine the blessings pictured here,
Thine are those charms that dazzle and endear;
Too blest, indeed, were such without alloy,
But, fostered e'en by freedom, ills annoy;
That independence Britons prize too high,
Keeps man from man, and breaks the social tie:
The self-dependent lordlings stand alone,
All claims that bind and sweeten life unknown.
Here, by the bonds of nature feebly held,
Minds combat minds, repelling and repelled;
Ferments arise, imprisoned factions roar,
Represt ambition struggles round her shore,
Till, overwrought, the general system feels
Its motions stop, or frenzy fire the wheels.

Nor this the worst. As nature's ties decay,
As duty, love, and honor fail to sway,
Fictitious bonds, the bonds of wealth and law,
Still gather strength, and force unwilling awe.
Hence all obedience bows to these alone,
And talent sinks, and merit weeps unknown;
Till time may come, when, stripped of all her charms,
The land of scholars, and the nurse of arms,
Where noble stems transmit the patriot flame,
Where kings have toiled, and poets wrote for fame,
One sink of level avarice shall lie,
And scholars, soldiers, kings, unhonored die.

Yet think not, thus when freedom's ills I state,
I mean to flatter kings, or court the great.
Ye powers of truth, that bid my soul aspire,
Far from my bosom drive the low desire!
And thou, fair Freedom, taught alike to feel
The rabble's rage, and tyrant's angry steel;
Thou transitory flower, alike undone
By proud contempt, or favor's fostering sun,
Still may thy blooms the changeful clime endure!
I only would repress them to secure.

41

For just experience tells, in every soil,
That those who think must govern those that toil;
And all that freedom's highest aims can reach
Is but to lay proportioned loads on each.
Hence, should one order disproportioned grow,
Its double weight must ruin all below.

  Oh, then, how blind to all that truth requires,
Who think it freedom when a part aspires!
Calm is my soul, nor apt to rise in arms,
Except when fast-approaching danger warms;
But when contending chiefs blockade the throne,
Contracting regal power to stretch their own,
When I behold a factious band agree
To call it freedom when themselves are free;
Each wanton judge new penal statutes draw,
Laws grind the poor, and rich men rule the law;
The wealth of climes where savage nations roam
Pillaged from slaves to purchase slaves at home;
Fear, pity, justice, indignation start,
Tear off reserve, and bare my swelling heart;
Till, half a patriot, half a coward grown,
I fly from petty tyrants to the throne.

43

Yes, brother, curse with me that baleful hour
When first ambition struck at regal power,
And, thus polluting honor in its source,
Gave wealth to sway the mind with double force.
Have we not seen, round Britain's peopled shore,
Her useful sons exchanged for useless ore?
Seen all her triumphs but destruction haste,
Like flaring tapers brightening as they waste?
Seen opulence, her grandeur to maintain,
Lead stern depopulation in her train,
And, over fields where scattered hamlets rose,
In barren solitary pomp repose?
Have we not seen, at pleasure's lordly call,
The smiling, long-frequented village fall?
Beheld the duteous son, the sire decayed,
The modest matron, and the blushing maid,
Forced from their homes, a melancholy train,
To traverse climes beyond the western main,
Where wild Oswego spreads her swamps around,
And Niagara stuns with thundering sound?

E'en now, perhaps, as there some pilgrim strays
Through tangled forests and through dangerous ways,
Where beasts with man divided empire claim,

45

And the brown Indian marks with murderous aim;
There, while above the giddy tempest flies,
And all around distressful yells arise,
The pensive exile, bending with his woe,
To stop too fearful, and too faint to go,
Casts a long look where England's glories shine,
And bids his bosom sympathize with mine.

Vain, very vain, my weary search to find
That bliss which only centres in the mind.
Why have I strayed from pleasure and repose,
To seek a good each government bestows?
In every government, though terrors reign,
Though tyrant kings or tyrant laws restrain,
How small, of all that human hearts endure,
That part which laws or kings can cause or cure!
Still to ourselves in every place consigned,
Our own felicity we make or find.
With secret course, which no loud storms annoy,
Glides the smooth current of domestic joy;
The lifted axe, the agonizing wheel,
Luke's iron crown, and Damiens' bed of steel,
To men remote from power but rarely known,
Leave reason, faith, and conscience, all our own.

47